KITTENS

Rand McNally & Company
Chicago • New York • San Francisco

I wonder what
all the fuss
is about . . .
haven't they
ever seen
a folding chair
before?

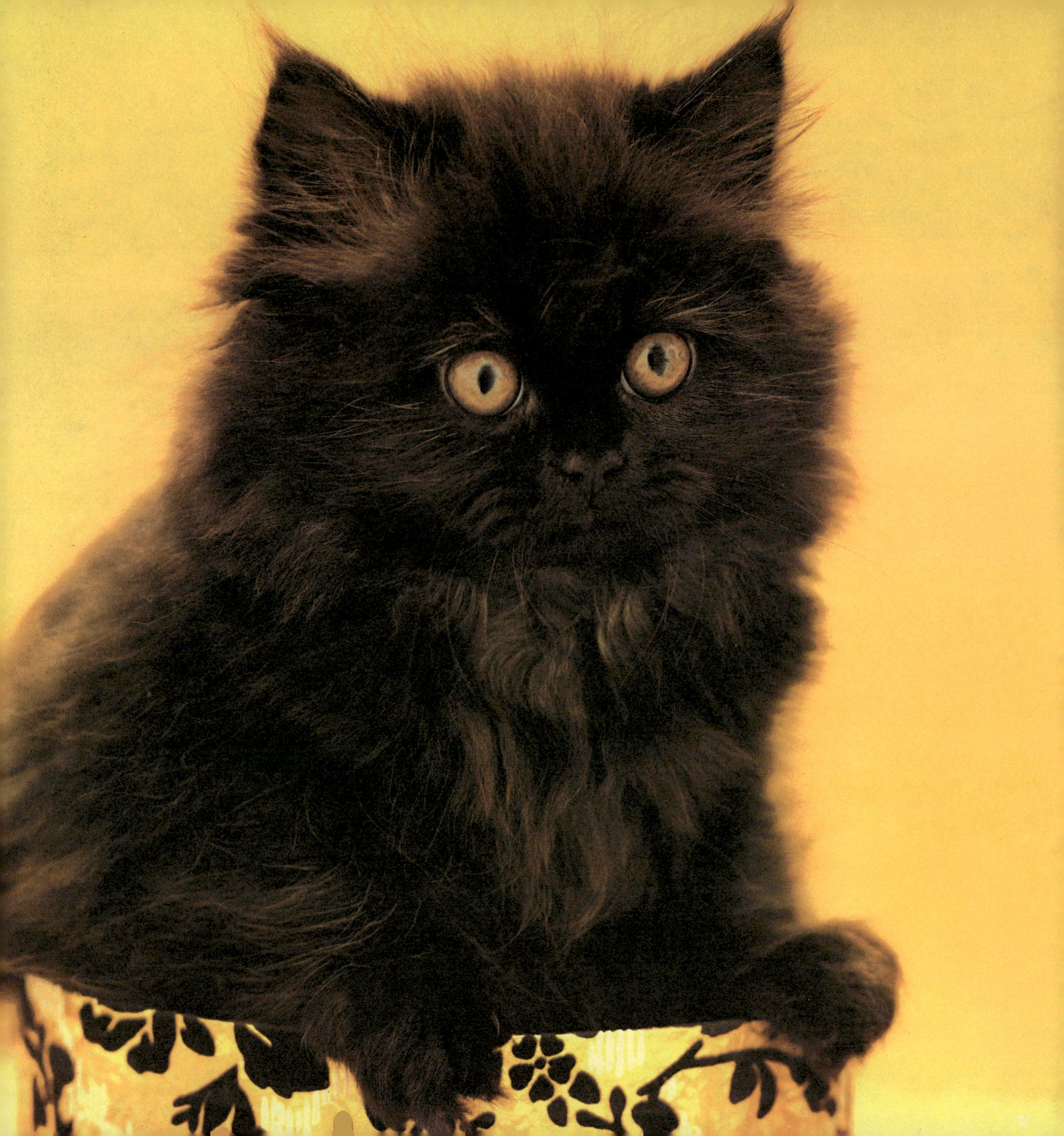

Look,
there's a new kitty.
What beautiful brown
eyes she has!

Yes, and such
fluffy brown fur!

Please come and pull our wagon. We want to go for a ride.

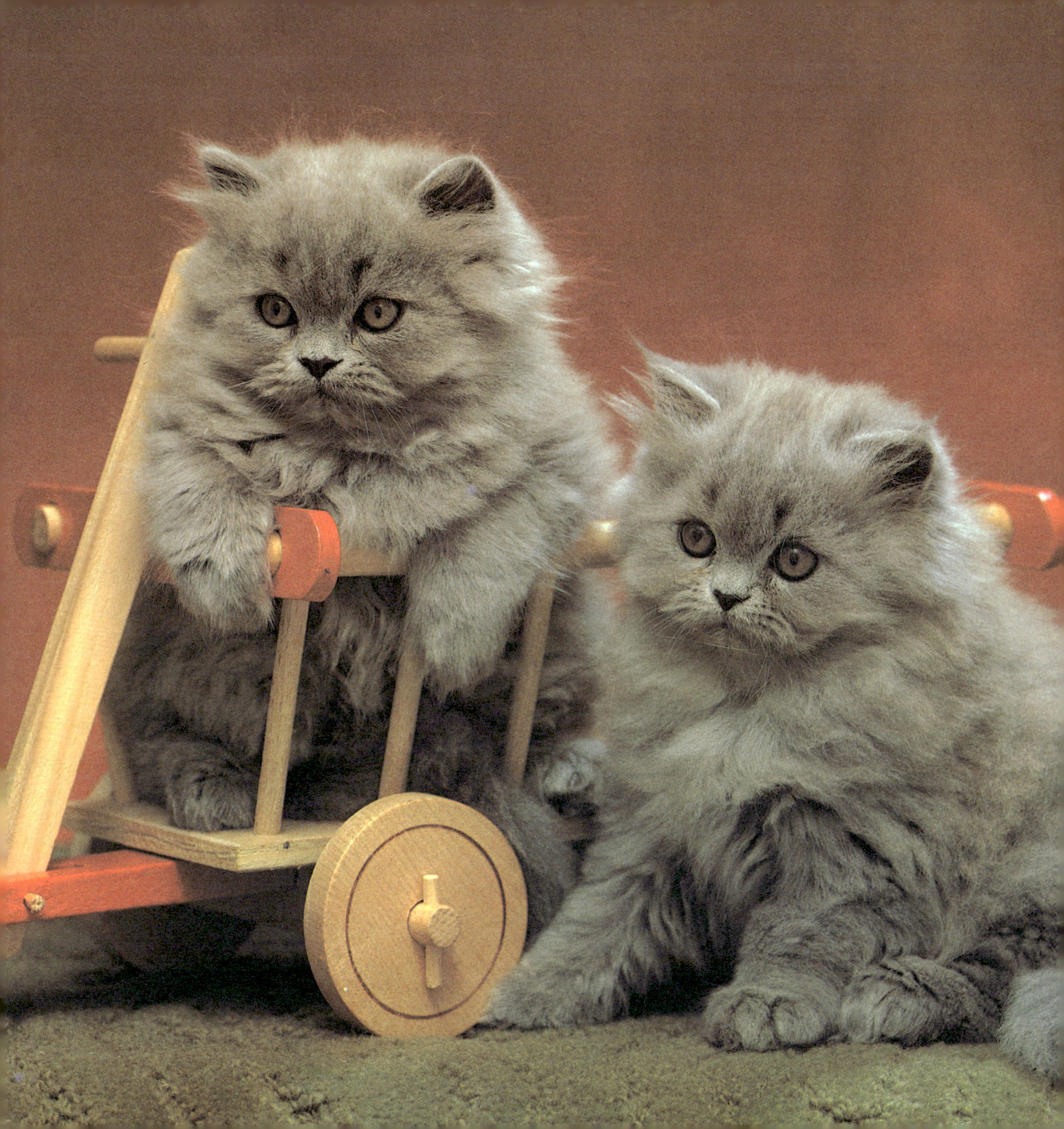

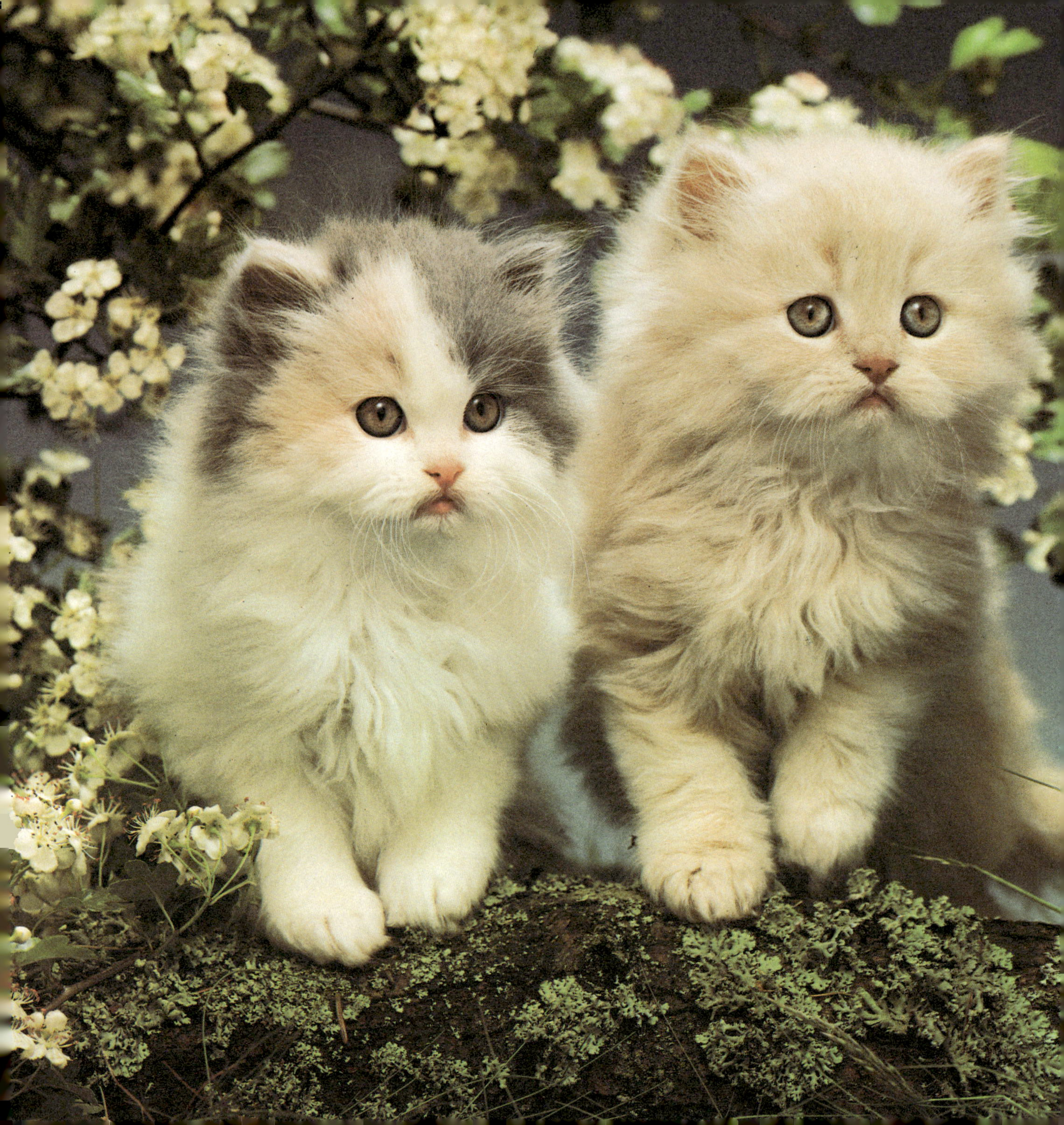

We kittens
mee-ow and scamper
about and blink
our eyes.
But Bear just sits
and won't play
with us.

Oh, dear! Oh, dear!
Has anyone seen
our baby kitten?

We have;
she's right there
on the grass.

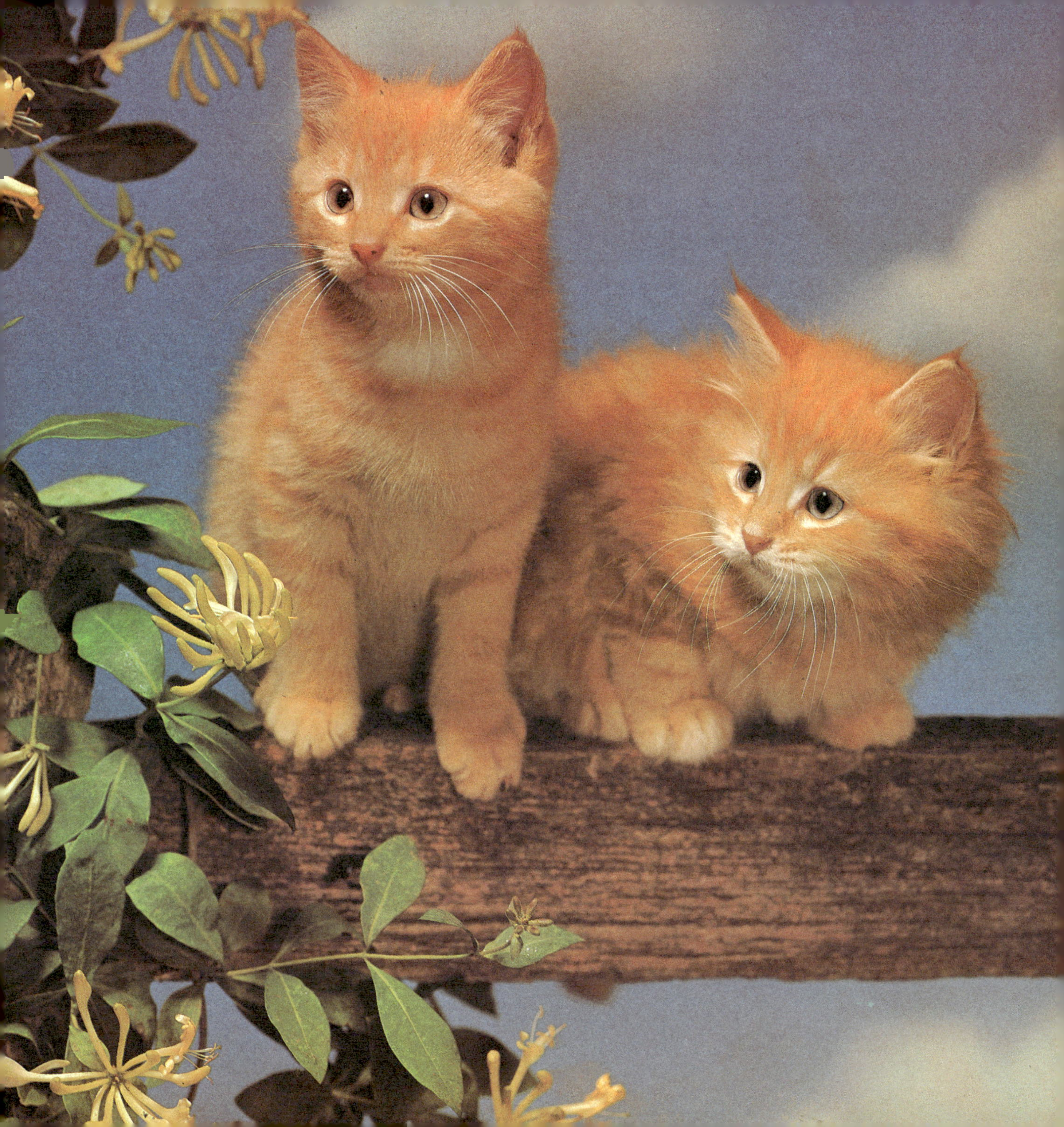

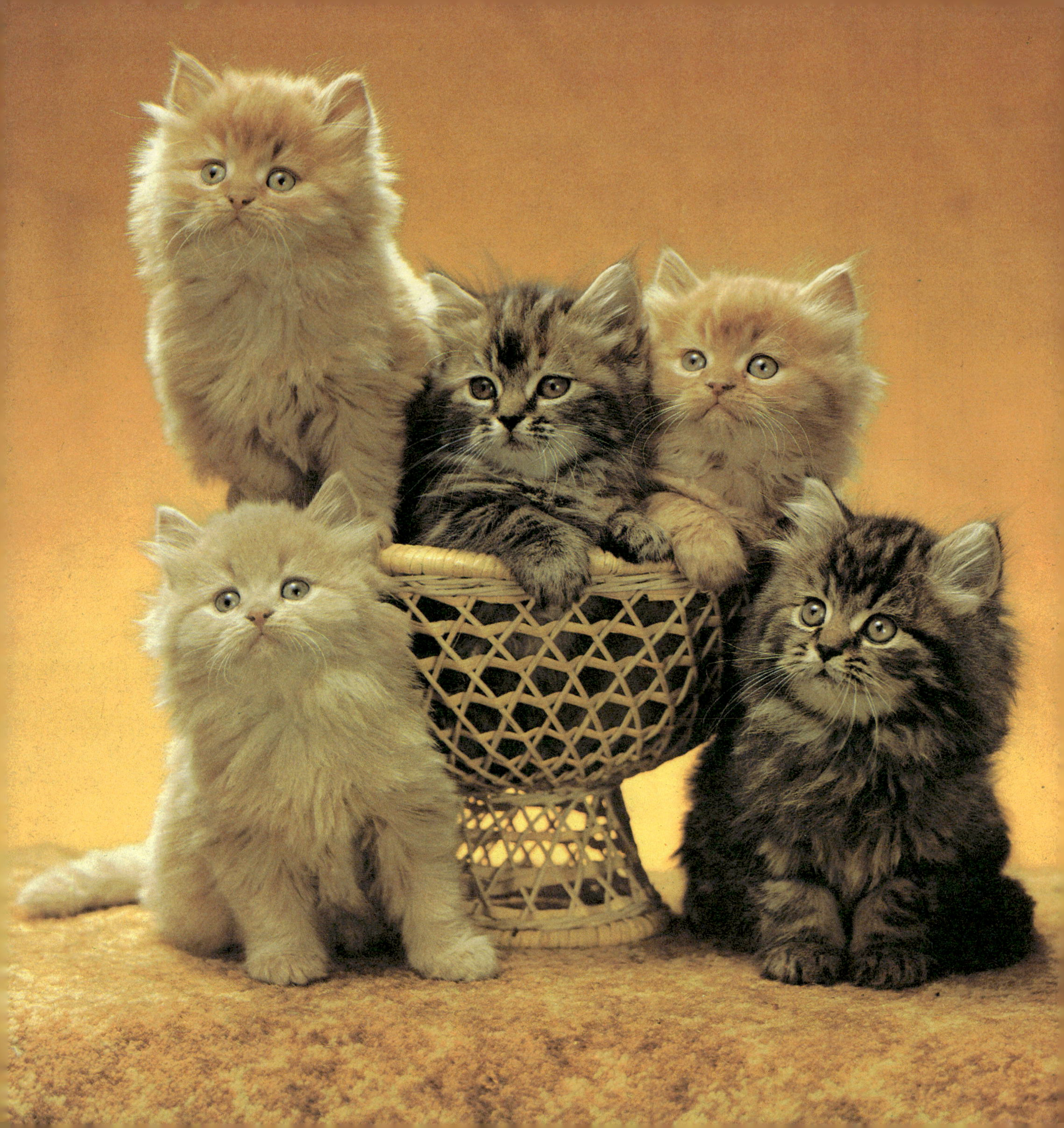

This basket
isn't big enough
to hold five kitties.
Can't you see that
we need more room?

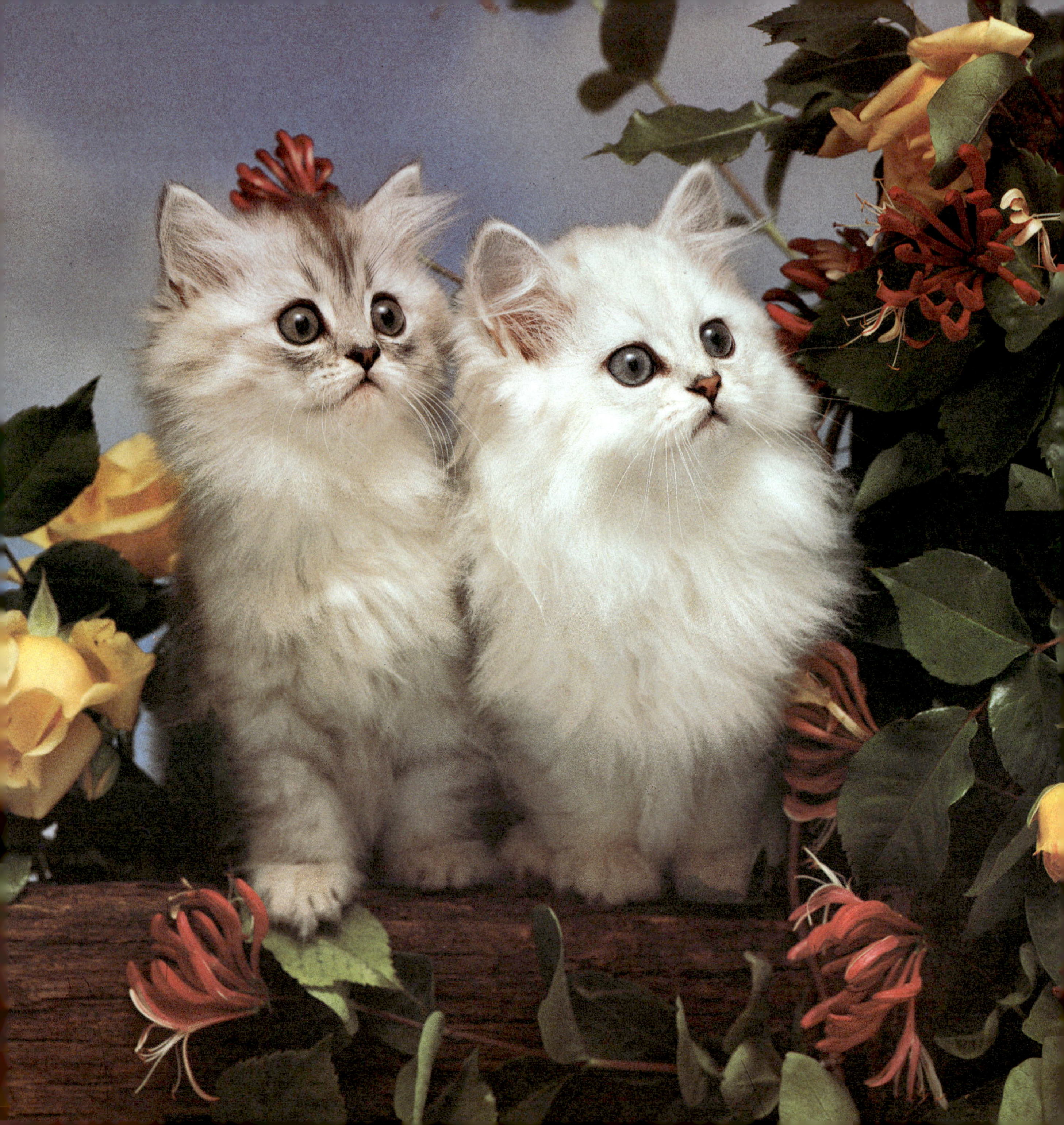

Flowers are so pretty to look at. Which color do you like best?

I love trinkets
and beads.
Ah, a long chain
of pearls . . .
let's play.

Okay, we're ready!

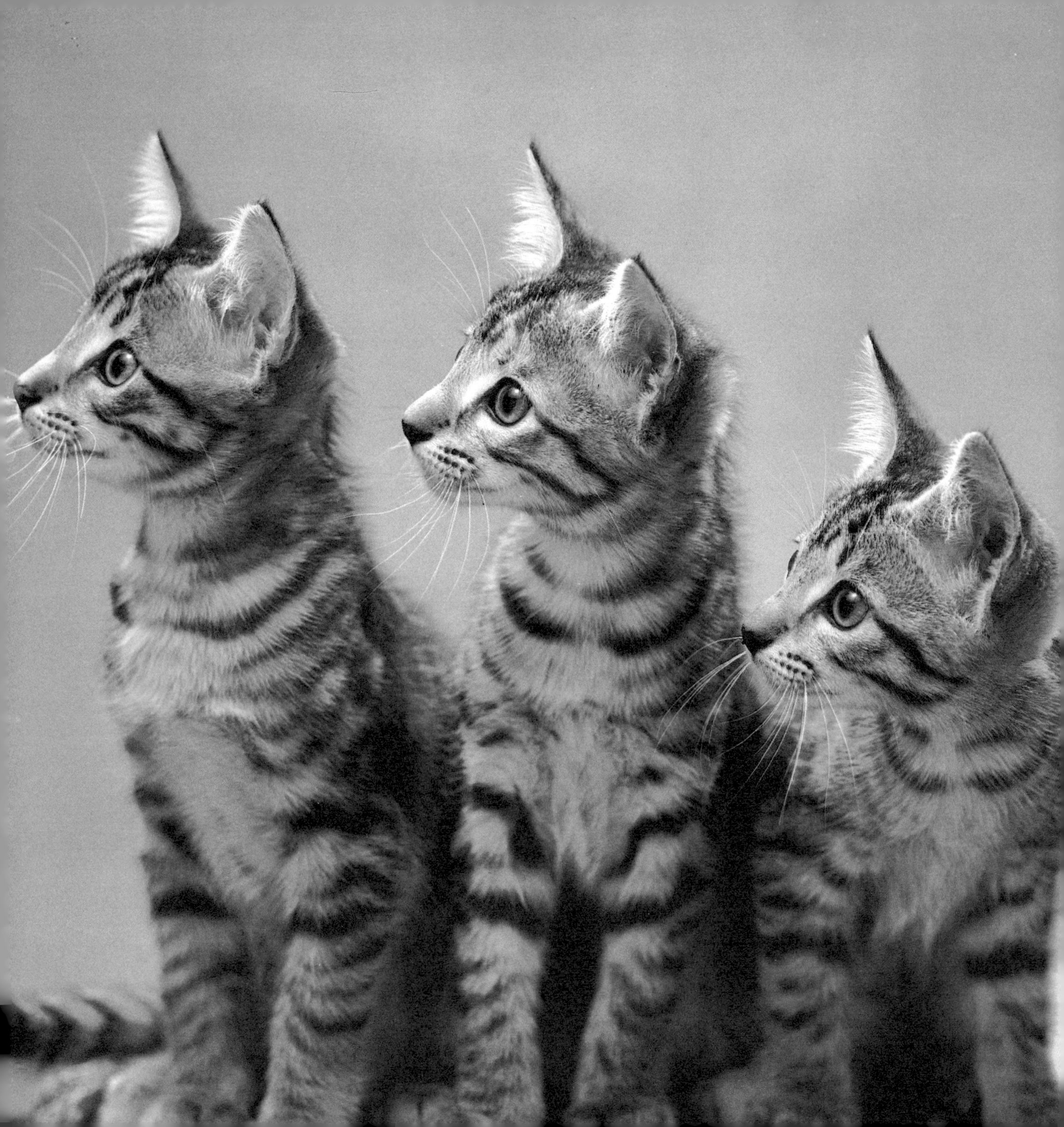

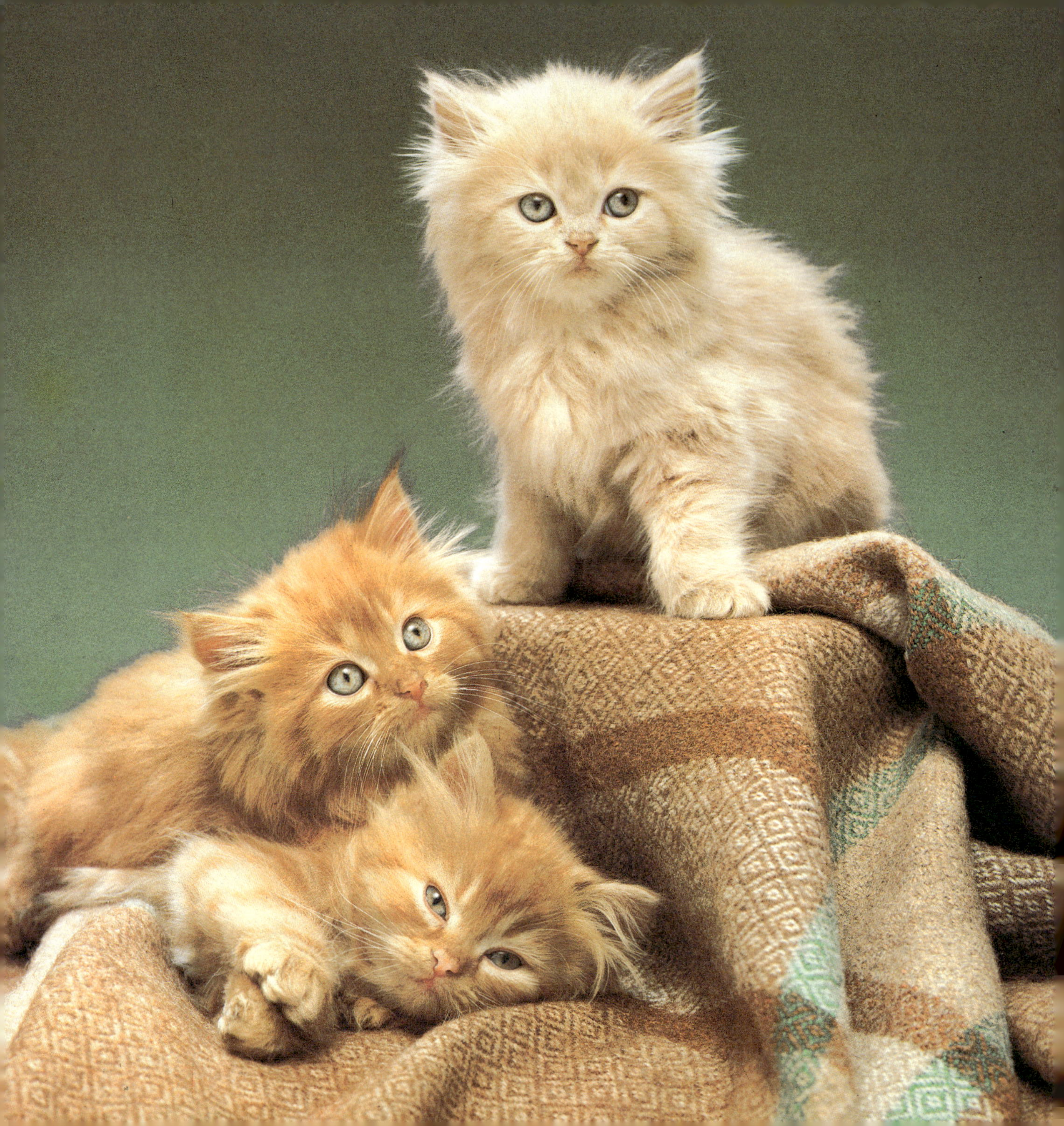

What do you think these kittens are looking at? It may be a little sparrow. Or is it a big, fat robin?

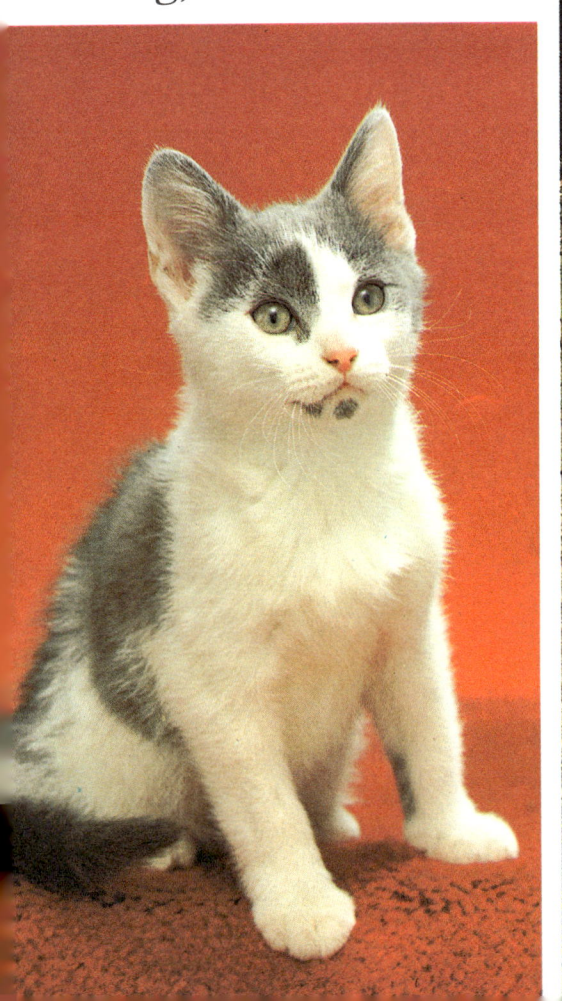

Holly and mistletoe — Christmas will soon be here!

Don't you wish
that you had
a nice swing like ours?
If you give us a push,
then we'll give
you a ride.

Copyright © 1983 Colour Library Books Ltd.
Text copyright © 1984 Rand McNally & Company.
All rights reserved. Printed in U.S.A.
Library of Congress Catalog Card Number: 83-63588